KU-395-639

OCTOPUSES

Darlene R. Stille

www.heinemann.co.uk
Visit our website to find out more information about Heinemann Library books.

To order:
☎ Phone 44 (0) 1865 888066
▤ Send a fax to 44 (0) 1865 314091
▢ Visit the Heinemann Bookshop at www.heinemann.co.uk to browse our catalogue and order online.

First published in Great Britain by Heinemann Library,
Halley Court, Jordan Hill, Oxford OX2 8EJ,
part of Harcourt Education Ltd.
Heinemann is a registered trademark of Harcourt
Education Ltd.

Edited by Barbara Katz, Kathy Peltan
Designed by Kimberly Saar, Heinemann Library
Illustrations and maps by John Fleck
Photo research by Bill Broyles
Production by John Nelson and Viv Hichens
Originated by Ambassador Litho Ltd.
Printed by Wing King Tong in Hong Kong

ISBN 0431 18200 0
07 06 05 04 03
10 9 8 7 6 5 4 3 2 1

British Library Cataloguing in Publication Data
Stille, Darlene R.
Octopuses. - (Sea creatures)
594.5'6
A full catalogue record for this book is available from
the British Library.

Acknowledgments
The author and publishers are grateful to the
following for permission to reproduce copyright
material:
Cover photograph by David B. Fleetham/Seapics.com

Title page, icons Art Womack/Pictor International;
pp. 4, 27 Jeffrey Rotman/Seapics.com; pp. 5, 23 Bob
Cranston/Seapics.com; pp. 6, 15B, 29 Doug
Perrine/Seapics.com; pp. 8, 20 David B.
Fleetham/Seapics.com; p. 9 Gregory
Ochocki/Seapics.com; pp. 10, 12 Norbert Wu
Photography; p. 11 David J. Wrobel/Monterey Bay
Aquarium Foundation; pp. 13, 18 Fred Bavendam/
Minden Pictures; p. 14 Mike Severns/Seapics.com;
pp. 15T, 19 Clay Bryce/Seapics.com; p. 16 Brandon D.
Cole; p. 17 Masa Ushioda/Seapics.com; p. 21 A. & C.
Mahaney/Seapics.com; p. 22 Dr. James B. Wood;
p. 24 Flip Nicklin/Minden Pictures; p. 25 Glen M.
Oliver/Visuals Unlimited; p. 26 Robert F. Sisson/
National Geographic Society; p. 26 Visuals Unlimited;
p. 28 Brandon D. Cole

Special thanks to Dr James Woods of the National
Resource Center of Cephalopods in Galveston, Texas,
and to Michael Bright, Executive Producer, BBC
Natural History Unit for their help in the preparation
of this book.

Every effort has been made to contact copyright
holders of any material reproduced in this book.
Any omissions will be rectified in subsequent printings
if notice is given to the publishers.

Contents

You can find words in bold, **like this**, in the Glossary.

How would you find a giant octopus?

You join a team of scientists, called marine biologists, who study octopuses in the Pacific Ocean. They know that some of the huge animals live off the coast of Oregon, USA.

You need the right equipment

You travel by boat to a place that the marine biologists know is home to some octopuses. You put on a tight-fitting wet suit made of a rubbery material that will keep your body warm in the cold water. After a final check of your **SCUBA** gear, you put the air tank on your back like a backpack. SCUBA stands for Self-Contained Underwater Breathing Apparatus. The metal tank is filled with a mixture of gases that take the place of the air you normally breathe. A hose connects the tank to a mouthpiece so that you can breathe underwater.

A scientist diving in the deep, cold waters of the northern Pacific Ocean comes face to face with a giant Pacific octopus. If the diver leaves the octopus alone, he has nothing to fear.

A glass diving mask covers your eyes so you can see underwater. Rubber fins on your feet help you swim. Your team members carry bright lights to help you see in the dark water. You are diving at night, when octopuses come out to feed.

You need to be in the right place

You jump into the water and slowly sink towards the seabed. Near the bottom, everyone stops. Right below you is an amazing sight. It looks like a leather bag with eight long arms. It is a giant Pacific octopus.

Suddenly, the giant octopus turns its big eyes towards you. Will those long arms reach out like a monster in a story and grab you? Don't worry. The giant Pacific octopus, like all octopuses, is very shy. It squirts a cloud of dark **ink** at you and disappears into the darkness.

Is it a head or a body?

The octopus's 'body' looks as if it should be the head. The head is where you might think the body begins. A giant Pacific octopus looks like a big, soft round bean bag crawling around on the seabed.

It's a headfoot

The octopus is a kind of animal called a **cephalopod**. The word *cephalopod* comes from Greek words that mean 'head' and 'foot'. Squid and cuttlefish are also cephalopods.

Cephalopods belong to a group of animals called **molluscs**. Molluscs are **invertebrates**, animals that do not have backbones. In fact, molluscs do not have any bones at all. Some molluscs have shells to protect their soft bodies. Clams and snails are molluscs that have hard, outer shells. The octopus does not have a shell.

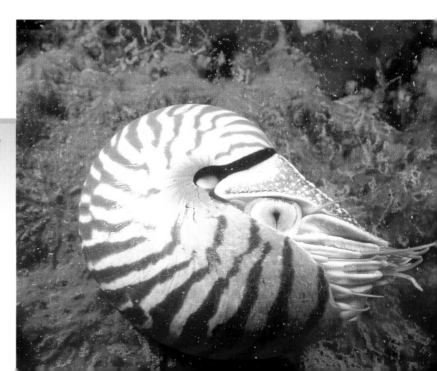

The chambered nautilus is a relative of the octopus.

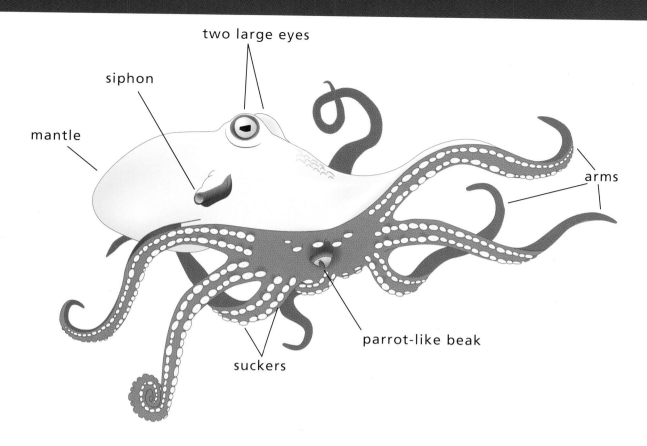

two large eyes

siphon

mantle

arms

parrot-like beak

suckers

It's a bag without bones

The bag-like structure is called the **mantle**. This is the
octopus's 'body'. It is made of muscle and is the only thing
that protects the soft internal organs. Two eyes sit just
below the mantle. The area between the eyes is the head.
This is where the brain is.

The mantle contains the octopus's heart, digestive system
and other internal organs. Between the inside of the bag
and the internal organs, there is a space called the **mantle
cavity**. The octopus has **gills** inside the mantle cavity. Fish
and almost all other animals that spend their lives in the
water use gills to breathe. The octopus sucks water into the
cavity through slits in the mantle. The gills take oxygen from
this water and send it to the octopus's blood.

The octopus has lots of heart

An octopus has three hearts. A heart at the end of each **gill** takes in blood from tiny blood vessels. As the blood is pumped through the gills, it picks up oxygen from the water. The third heart then gets this blood and pumps it through the octopus's body.

After the gills take oxygen from the water, muscles in the **mantle** force the water back out through a tube called a **siphon**. Then the gills take in a fresh supply of water with oxygen.

It has amazing arms

An octopus's arms bend and twist in all directions. One or two rows of powerful **suckers** cover the underside of each arm. These can hold on to rocks. Octopuses that live on the seabed use their arms to crawl along, into cracks and under rocks.

Each sucker has special nerve cells called **chemoreceptors**. The chemoreceptors sense substances in the water, just as our noses sense substances in the air. The suckers also let the octopus feel and taste the world around it.

The eight arms of an octopus join together under the mantle around the octopus's mouth.

Each arm is covered with suckers that look like suction cups. The powerful suckers can grab rocks or hold on to prey. The suckers can also feel, taste and smell.

An octopus's web

An octopus's arms are made mostly of muscle. They are connected under the mantle by a piece of skin called the **webbing**. In the centre of the webbing is the octopus's mouth. The mouth is a hard, sharp **beak** that looks like the beak of a parrot.

True blue

An octopus's blood is blue, not red. Human blood is red because it contains haemoglobin, which turns red when it attaches to the oxygen it carries to the body's cells. Octopus blood has a substance called haemocyanin, which does not bind, or connect, as easily to oxygen.

How many kinds of octopus are there?

It can be hard to find octopuses, but scientists think there are about 150 different kinds. New **species** are still being discovered. The waters off Australia may have more kinds of octopus than anywhere else in the world.

The common octopus

There really is an octopus species called the common octopus. It lives all over the world in warm waters, including those around the southern half of the British Isles. The curled octopus and the lesser octopus also live near Britain. They are closely related. The lesser octopus is a particularly good swimmer. All these octopuses belong to a group called the incirrata.

This Californian octopus, from arm tip to arm tip, is smaller than your little finger.

A giant Pacific octopus can be a scary sight. Its arms are long enough to wrap around a car. The giant Pacific octopus is the largest octopus known.

Unusual octopuses

Octopuses in the cirrata group live in the open sea as far down as 5 kilometres. They have **webbing** that starts at the **mantle** and goes almost to the tips of their arms. The extra webbing gives cirrate octopuses a bell shape. They also have two small fins on their mantle. Scientists do not know very much about **cirrate** octopuses. They are hard to find and study.

This cirrate octopus looks like a big hat. Cirrate octopuses have cirri on their arms instead of suckers. These are rows of thin, hair-like organs.

Where do octopuses live?

Octopuses live in the salty water of seas and oceans all over the world. Some are **benthic.** That means they live on the seabed. Others are **pelagic** and float in the open sea at different depths.

Benthic habitats

The sea has different depths at different places. The sea is shallower near the coast. A coastal benthic octopus might live at a depth of 200 metres. That's the length of four Olympic swimming pools. But far out at sea, the bottom may be as deep as 1000 metres.

Benthic waters can be warm or cold. The giant Pacific octopus is a cold-water benthic **species** that lives out at sea. Some common octopuses live in shallow water off the coast of Florida, where the water is warmer.

This is an Antarctic octopus. This very small species lives only in the southern hemisphere. It eats tiny shrimp and other crustaceans.

A tin can or a broken bottle can make a snug, safe den for an octopus. An octopus may also move into an empty den that was built by another octopus.

Pelagic habitats

Any water that is not near the shore is pelagic, or open sea water. These waters are usually cold. Pelagic octopus species can also be found at different depths. Many of the **cirrate** octopuses are pelagic.

Visiting an octopus's home

Most octopuses build their homes on the mud, sand or gravel of the seabed. An octopus's home is called a **den**. The den might be a hole under a rock or in a pile of rocks. Octopuses like a den with an opening that is hard to get into. Small octopuses have even been known to make use of a rusty tin can or an old bucket for a den. Anywhere that an octopus can crawl into and hide makes a good home.

? Did you know?

An octopus can squeeze through a hole as small as its beak.

What does an octopus eat?

The octopus is a **predator.** It eats other animals. The octopus hunts mainly at night.

Octopuses love seafood

The favourite foods of an octopus are fish, clams, crabs, shrimps and snails. Except for fish, these sea animals have hard shells, but that is not a problem for an octopus. Sometimes the octopus uses its arms and suckers to pull the shell apart.

An octopus can also use its sharp **beak** to break the shell or to punch a hole in the shell. It can drill a hole in the shell with its strange tongue, called a **radula**. The radula is covered with tiny, rough teeth. Then the octopus puts its saliva, which contains a poison, into the shell. The poison makes it difficult for the **prey** to keep moving, so it is easier for the octopus to eat it.

Octopus rubbish

After an octopus has eaten, it puts the shells just outside the opening of its **den.** The shells pile up in a heap called a **midden**. Divers looking for octopus dens look for middens.

*An octopus grabs a **mollusc** with its suckers and tucks the animal under its mantle.*

Middens help scientists learn what an octopus has been eating.

The long, snake-like body of the moray eel can squeeze inside the den of an octopus.

Some animals like to eat octopuses!

Many animals like to eat octopus. Octopuses provide food for seals, whales, sharks and other large fish and moray eels. Only larger predators can catch a large octopus.

Octopuses also provide food for people. Divers use spear guns to hunt octopus. Octopuses are sometimes caught with fishing lures and in nets or traps. Cooks use the **mantle** and arms of an octopus in recipes. Sometimes they fry the octopus. Sometimes they use octopus in sauces. People have been eating octopus for thousands of years.

How does an octopus protect itself?

One way for an octopus to keep safe is to use **camouflage** and 'disappear'. Another way is to be alert and to avoid danger. Octopuses also have other methods of defence.

Mimicry is a type of camouflage. The mimic octopus was discovered in 1998. This one has shaped its body like a mantis shrimp.

It is a master of disguise

Octopuses can use **cryptic camouflage** to hide from **predators.** They change their skin colour and texture to match their **habitat.** Some octopuses can do this in only a second. Special cells in their skin, called **chromatophores,** make it possible for octopuses to change colour. An octopus can have hundreds of chromatophores in an area of skin no bigger than the tip of a pencil rubber.

Special muscles let an octopus fold its skin to look rough, like rocks, or smooth, like sand. An angry octopus can make the skin on top of its **mantle** stick up to look like horns.

The Caribbean reef octopus can make itself blend in with the colours of a coral reef.

An octopus squirts a cloud of dark ink into the water.
The diver has annoyed the octopus by holding on to it.

It confuses the enemy

Another octopus trick is to send out a cloud of dark **ink**. Inside an octopus's mantle is an organ called an ink sac. The sac contains ink that is usually coloured black or dark brown. If a predator, such as a shark, is after an octopus, the octopus can squirt ink out of its ink sac.

The ink mixes with the water to create a dark cloud around the octopus. Sometimes the ink cloud takes on the shape of the octopus's body. The shark cannot see the octopus because of the dark ink cloud. The shark becomes confused. This gives the octopus time to get away.

17

An octopus *is* always alert

An octopus cannot hear (no ears!), but its body can feel vibrations. It can feel the vibrations of a boat, a swimmer or a **predator** coming towards it. If an octopus feels threatened, it first tries to hide in its **den** or in the crack of a rock.

The octopus can raise its eyes up above its **mantle** like two stalks. This lets the octopus peek outside its den without exposing its body. Sometimes it just raises up one eye. Octopuses can see objects as well as you can, but they cannot see colours. However, octopuses can see very well at night.

A giant Pacific octopus props itself up to take a look around.

The deadly blue-ringed octopus has colourful blue rings all over its body. It also has venom, or poison, that can kill a human being.

Protection by attracting attention

Like all octopuses, the blue-ringed octopus from Australia is shy and will hide when people or predators appear. But if it feels threatened, bright blue rings flash across its skin. These rings mean 'Stay away or else!'

Swimmers and divers should never try to pick up a blue-ringed octopus or pull the octopus from its den. The blue-ringed octopus can bite and inject a powerful venom, or poison. A small amount of this venom is strong enough to kill several average-size adults!

Jetting away

When it is in great danger, the octopus does not use its arms to crawl away. The octopus makes its body behave like the engine of a jet plane. A jet takes in air and shoots it out of the back of the engine. The octopus does the same with water.

First, the octopus takes in water through the two slits in its head. The water fills the **mantle cavity.** Then the octopus uses the muscles of its **mantle** to push the water out of its **siphon.** A jet of water shoots backwards out of the octopus. The force of the jet pushes the octopus forwards. With its long arms trailing behind, the octopus jets away to the safety of a hole in a rock or its **den.**

*If an octopus cannot avoid a **predator** by hiding, using camouflage, or shooting **ink** it will try to escape by jetting away. This is a day octopus.*

Does an octopus have a family?

There is no such thing as an octopus family of mother, father and little octopuses. Every octopus lives by itself in its own den.

A male mates with a female octopus. The octopus reproduces through sexual reproduction.

The octopus *is* a loner

Octopuses do not get together very much. They live alone, hunt alone and eat alone.

Scientists once thought that octopuses never gathered together in groups. Then some scientists reported that they had seen young red octopuses in a group called a **school.** Fish often gather in schools for protection. That may be why the red octopuses did it. No one knows for sure. The red octopus is the only type of octopus that scientists have seen in schools, but other types may do it too.

Octopuses do get together to mate

Octopuses reproduce sexually. Sperm from a male octopus must fertilize the eggs of a female octopus.

The male octopus has a special arm used for mating. This arm is shorter than his other seven arms. The male octopus uses his short arm to place a packet of sperm inside the mantle of a female octopus.

Each egg has lots of company

The female uses the sperm to fertilize her eggs. She strings the eggs together. Then she hangs the strings of eggs in her **den**. The tiny dwarf octopus hangs hundreds of eggs and may use an empty clam shell for a den. A big octopus may hang thousands of eggs inside her den of rocks.

An octopus egg does not have a hard shell like the egg of a chicken. The shell is soft and transparent. This means you can see the little octopus inside the see-through egg.

A mother devoted to caring for eggs

A little octopus begins to grow inside each egg. The mother spends all her time taking care of the eggs. She guards them from **predators**, such as starfish, that try to get into the den and eat the eggs. Even though the eggs are already underwater, she sprays them with more water to keep them clean and give them more oxygen.

The egg is soft and clear. You can see the baby octopus inside.

The giant Pacific octopus hangs her eggs inside her den. The mother spends all her time caring for the eggs. After the eggs hatch, the mother dies.

The mother octopus does not eat while she takes care of the eggs. She does not even sleep. When the baby octopuses hatch out of their eggs, the mother dies. Each baby octopus is then on its own.

The babies have to take care of themselves.

A newborn octopus looks like an adult octopus, only much smaller. It can do everything an adult can do. It can change colour. It can even squirt **ink**.

It is very important for a baby octopus not to be seen by anything that might eat it. The newborn octopuses swim to the surface of the water. They float around with lots of tiny plants and other small animals called **plankton**.

Many baby octopuses are eaten by bigger animals. The ones that survive settle to the bottom and grow up. They find an empty **den** or build a new one. They live alone until they **mate**, and then they die.

An octopus's life is short

Octopuses do not live very long. Small warm-water octopuses live for about a year. Big octopuses, such as the giant Pacific octopus, usually live for three years.

The eight arms can be clearly seen on this newly hatched baby octopus.

Are octopuses endangered?

No octopus **species** is on the list of **endangered** animals. But no one really knows for sure if they are safe.

No one knows for sure

It is very difficult to study octopuses. They are shy and hard to find and so are not easy to count. Scientists do not even know for sure how many species there are. They think there are about 150 octopus species worldwide.

A dead octopus lies on a beach. No one knows for sure whether any species of octopus is endangered.

Could octopuses ever become endangered?

A species of octopus could become endangered if the octopuses die faster than they can reproduce. Sea pollution that harms its **habitat** or kills the octopus's **prey** is also a concern.

Many people like to eat octopuses, but it is important not to catch too many. People who work in the pet trade like to catch the more attractive octopus species. This can also reduce the numbers of octopuses.

How do we learn about octopuses?

Marine biologists observe octopuses that live in public **aquariums**, study them in laboratories and try to find them in the sea.

Studying octopuses in the sea

Most scientists study octopuses in the sea. They put on **SCUBA** gear and dive down to study how octopuses live in shallow water. They use little submarines to study octopuses that live in deep water. Sometimes scientists use robot submarines called **ROVs**. ROV stands for Remotely Operated Vehicle. ROVs have found out new things about octopuses.

Not all octopuses live on the seabed. Some octopuses float in the middle of the sea. These octopuses do not live in **dens**. So they cannot lay eggs in dens. The female lays eggs under her long arms!

Scientists use ROVs to look for octopuses that live too deep for divers to go.

*The common blanket octopus lives in the Mediterranean Sea and along both coasts of the North and South Atlantic Ocean. Scientists do not know much about this **species**.*

Scientists need to learn more about octopuses. They want to know how many there are. Do all octopuses always live alone? How strong is the biggest octopus? How clever is the average octopus? There is much more to discover about these wonderful creatures of the sea.

Studying octopuses in the laboratory

Scientists agree that the octopus is the most advanced **invertebrate**. They are clever, but not in the same way that humans are clever. There have been some experiments to see if octopuses can learn by watching other octopuses do things, such as opening jars. Some scientists think the results show that octopuses can learn by watching. Others feel that more experiments are needed.

☑ The largest octopus is the giant octopus that lives in the Pacific Ocean. It can weigh up to 68 kilograms – that is as much as an adult human being weighs. The distance from the tip of one arm to the tip of another can be 7.5 metres. Its arms are big enough to hug a car.

☑ The longer its arms, the more suckers an octopus has. The adult female giant Pacific octopus has a total of 2240 suckers, 280 on each arm. An adult male has fewer suckers, because one of its arms is used for mating and is shorter than the others.

☑ If an octopus loses an arm, it can grow a new one, complete with suckers.

☑ An octopus's oesophagus, or throat, goes through its brain.

☑ An octopus can be killed by its own **ink**. If an octopus in an **aquarium** squirts ink, the ink covers its gills and it cannot breathe. The water must be changed right away.

This octopus is using its arms to walk on the sea bottom.

- Long ago, octopus ink was used as ink for pens.

- Not all octopuses can squirt ink. Most deep-sea octopuses do not have ink sacs.

- The colour of an octopus can depend upon its mood. If an octopus turns white, it may be frightened. If it turns red, it may be angry.

- An octopus has twice as many nerves in its body as it has in its brain. This is because each sucker has nerves.

- The common octopus lays about 250,000 eggs—that is a quarter of a million eggs!

- An octopus has arms, not tentacles. Tentacles are used to catch **prey**. Some tentacles have claws or hooks. The squid is a **cephalopod** that has eight arms and two tentacles.

This is a common day octopus. The yellow 'tube' is the **siphon**.

This is the same octopus. It has changed its colour from white to brown in only a few seconds.

Glossary

aquarium tank where fish and other sea animals are kept

beak hard, sharp mouth of an octopus

benthic of the seabed

camouflage way an animal hides

cephalopod type of animal that includes octopus, squid, the chambered nautilus and cuttlefish. Cephalopods belong to another group of animals called molluscs.

chemoreceptors special nerve cells in an octopus's suckers that sense substances in the water

chromatophores special cells in the skin that let the octopus change its colour

cirrate octopus that has rows of thin, hair-like organs on its arms instead of suckers

cryptic camouflage hiding by looking like the surroundings

den home of an octopus. A den can be a crack in a rock, a hole in the sand or a space under a pile of rocks. A den can also be an empty seashell or an old can.

endangered in danger of dying out completely

gills organs that fish and most other sea animals use for breathing

habitat place where an animal lives

ink dark liquid that an octopus sends out from an ink sac in its body when it feels threatened

invertebrates animals that do not have back bones

mantle bag-like structure made of muscle that contains the heart, digestive system and other internal organs of an octopus and other cephalopods.

mantle cavity space between the inside of the mantle and the internal organs

mate when a male and female animal come together to make babies

midden pile of shells and other remains of animals an octopus has eaten and that it has left outside its den

mimicry looking and acting like something else. Mimicry is a form of camouflage.

mollusc kind of animal that does not have a backbone. Some molluscs, such as clams and snails, have shells to protect their soft bodies. Other molluscs, such as octopuses, do not have shells.

pelagic of the open sea

plankton tiny plants and animals that float near the surface of the sea

predator animal that hunts and eats other animals

prey animal that another animal hunts for food

radula the 'tongue' of an octopus. The radula is covered with tiny, rough teeth.

ROV (Remotely Operated Vehicle) small robot submarine that scientists use for learning about the deep sea

school group of fish or other sea creatures that swim together

SCUBA (Self-Contained Underwater Breathing Apparatus) mouthpiece, hose and air tanks. The tanks contain a mixture of gases so a diver can breathe underwater.

siphon tube inside the mantle that sends water out of the mantle cavity after the gills take oxygen from the water

species type of animal or plant

suckers round cups on the underside of an octopus's arm that grab objects and also feel and taste the objects. Suckers are like suction cups.

webbing or web piece of skin that joins the arms of an octopus together under the mantle

More books to read

The Earth Strikes Back: Water, Pamela Grant and Arthur Haswell (Belitha Press, 2000)

Awesome Oceans: Monsters of the Deep, Michael Bright (Aladdin, Watts, 2002).

Octopuses, Squids and Cuttlefish, Trudi Strain Trueit (Franklin Watts, 2002)

Index

Titles in the *Sea Creatures* series include:

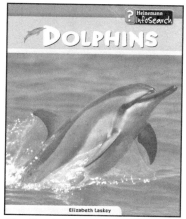

Hardback   0 431 18204 3

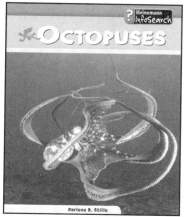

Hardback   0 431 18200 0

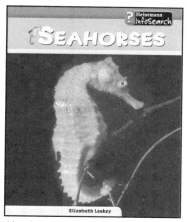

Hardback   0 431 18201 9

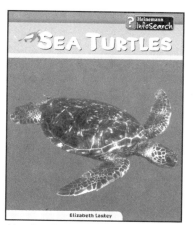

Hardback   0 431 18205 1

Hardback   0 431 18203 5

Hardback   0 431 18202 7

Find out about the other titles in this series on our website www.heinemann.co.uk/library